Hustling: From Heroin to Houses

By George Beatty

Dedication

For my Mom and Dad. You're not going to like all the stories in this book, but I love you, and I love that you love me.

.

Table of Contents

Foreword

Technically people from Dallas and people from Philly are not supposed to be friends. There's this decades' long rivalry between our two football teams that's supposed to divide us. Good thing your boy George and I don't waste our time watching football because I'm proud to call Mr. Beatty my friend.

If there's one thing about Americans, it's that we love a good underdog story. What you're about to read, is the classic underdog story with a win at the end. What makes this story so unique is that this is George's story. George is a guy who has literally gone from heroin to hero. His remarkable journey and the lessons learned from it are unmatched.

I believe the purpose of this book is to motivate you to see that any situation that you're in or facing can be conquered if you choose to take action. George's story proves that no matter where you are in life, there's always a way to go up.

One of the great things about America is that anyone can truly be anything. One day, you can be a complete waste of space on this earth who's a burden to everyone around them.

The next day, you can decide that you're ready to become a winner and make it happen. There are no limits in this great country, and stories like George's prove it.

As you read this book, you'll be tempted to judge the author. I urge you to use this story not to judge but to gain inspiration. George has beaten a massive addiction, picked himself up by the bootstraps and created a real life for himself with an impressive income. He made a choice to become a winner, and he followed through with it.

Let me point out two crucial factors you need to know before you read the rest of this book:

First, it's not easy writing a book. I know; I've written eight so far. When this particular book was being written, George was a part of a group of 100 people who wanted to write a book. George and four others are the only ones who finished their books. Writing a book is hard, and it takes extreme dedication.

Second, writing a book that airs out your past dirty laundry, like this one, is even harder. You worry that people will judge you, distance themselves from you and all-out avoid you like the plague. It takes big nuts to tell the world you used to do drugs, live on the streets and be a loser. It's not like the average person wants that broadcasted.

George has pushed past both boundaries and produced this book for you. This isn't a book for him. He already knows the story; he lived it. This is his life. He wrote the book you hold in your hands for your benefit. The experiences and lessons George shares in the book are to help you avoid some of the pitfalls that George dug himself out of.

I'm proud to have been a part of this whole process, and I'm proud of my friend George Beatty for taking the time and discipline to write this book and share it all. It takes a special kind of person to care enough to reveal so much of themselves like GB. Enjoy this book and be sure to thank George for turning his weaknesses into your strengths.

Introduction

This isn't a "how to get rich in real estate" book. (Keep your eye on GeorgeBeatty.com for one of those). It's not self-help. This book isn't going waste time lecturing you on "how to turn your life around in 90 days" or any other kind of over-simplistic platitude. If you're looking for something to read that makes you go "Oh fuck, I so wanna take over the world right this very moment..." I honestly can't promise you that either.

What I can promise is an "exactly what happened" book. If you want the real story: the nitty-gritty, the ups, the downs, the oh-shit-how-did-you-even-get-through-that-and-live-to-tell-the-tale-knock-you-down-and-get-you-back-up kind of story, then this might be for you. I say "might" because I've found that some people are into my style, and some people aren't, and that's totally fine by me. You win some; you lose some, right?

What I don't want you thinking going into this book is that I'm a pie-in-the-sky, self-professed guru here to swoon you over by using a get-rich-quick story with a course for sale at the end, or that this is some kind of "Hey, pay attention to me; do what I did; look how cool I am" kind of thing.

No.

I simply want to tell my story, in the hopes that someone out there can relate and realize it *is* reasonable to expect a life full of possibilities after you've been through some shit. Even major shit. This book is for the person who's had a roller coaster of a life, who's gotten knocked off, and who now wants to hop back on and really make their time count.

Life's not fair, and nobody ever said it would be. For some, that's a blessing, and for others, it's a cure.

Most of the people mentioned in the first half of this book are now dead, in jail, or out on the streets living in a cardboard box. I've been to so many funerals where I've sat there wondering why I'd made it and they didn't.

Knowing in my heart that they had the same chance I did to get clean and be alive today for their families, but they didn't take it. One thing that's always apparent to me every time I put on that same black suit, white shirt, and black tie I wear

9

to each funeral is this: Some of us get another chance, and some of us don't. Some people even get more than two chances. Nobody really knows why. That's life.

Sometimes, even seemingly hard and uncomfortable things like life not being fair can be advantageous. If life was fair to me, I'd be dead. That's the truth! And my mother would be one of countless other mothers who mourn every single time they set the dinner table, and there's an empty plate. I was one of the lucky ones, and I got my second chance. Rest assured, I'm taking this life for all it's worth! We only get one life. It's unfair, and it's hard, and it's too fucking short, and it's sad sometimes looking at those empty plates—but it's ours. And in the end, it's all we've got. We can waste it by being in a box—whether it's a casket, one made of cardboard, or any other kind—or we can just hop on, and enjoy the ride.

Welcome to my ride.

Chapter 1: Wallingford Warriors

When I first tried heroin, it was a small line of crushed-up tan powder, dumped out of a baby blue wax bag with "Nengo" stamped on it. We used a razor to cut it up finely, so you could snort it better. See, more surface area is preferable when you're snorting something because it makes it easier for your body to absorb it through your mucous membrane ... which is what happens when you snort any substance. The line itself was on top of a cracked CD case. Maybe an AC/DC album. (I'd ask Shawn, but he died from an overdose). I honestly don't even like AC/DC, but I REALLY liked the line of heroin. It tasted like B vitamins, combined with another taste that is so bland and unique it doesn't compare to anything. It's like you might expect cumin to taste if it was mixed with the most incredible physical orgasm you could imagine ... but more on that story later.

*****

I was born in a small suburban town outside of Philadelphia, about 20 minutes away from the city. The only store in the town was a Wawa. Other than that, it was exactly like what you would see in a movie like *The Stepford Wives*. Cookie-cutter houses, everyone seemed to have a nice job and a normal life. My family was the same: mom, dad, sister. My parents are still together, and they have a nice home.

As a kid, my biggest memory was that no matter how old I was, I always had a creeping, piercing feeling of inadequacy and isolation.

I didn't know that that wasn't normal at the time. I thought everyone felt that way. As if they were constantly thinking everything they were doing was wrong. That there would be consistent second-guessing. They would also feel the unending fear of being "found out." *Found out for what*? I knew there was nothing to that thought. It was just the feeling of being abnormal manifested in me. I think my mom knew something wasn't quite right. She was always dragging me to shrinks, and they would put me on antidepressants and Adderall. I started taking those drugs when I was about eight years old. Adderall is like meth.

Let me tell you about my mom. She's the most amazing woman who's ever been in my life. (Hi Mom, I love you.) She can ALWAYS tell when something's off with me. But we did experience the flipside, too. She could never seem to tell how bad it was or what was actually going on. She just knew that something wasn't right. So, she did what she thought she was supposed to do and kept taking me to specialists. I was so young, and all fucked up in the head, and I didn't feel like I could trust ANYONE with anything. I imagined if I told people how unhappy I was, they would lock me up or send me to a psychiatrist. Those doctors and therapists never knew what the fuck was up anyway. They were adults driving Jaguars, and I was just a kid who wanted the regular brand of Captain Crunch instead of the generic Sergeant Sugar cereal.

I dealt with not knowing what was wrong and trying to get along in life the best I could, but I fought with my sister a lot. I fought with my mom a lot, and in general, my whole experience as a kid wasn't that great. Nobody hit me. Nobody said anything directly mean to me. But a lot of emotional instability always surrounded my home life.

We went to Disneyland when I was young, and I know it is supposed to be the most magical place on earth. That wasn't my experience. My mom got lost, and my sister and my dad were fighting, as they were looking for Mom. I was soaking wet and cold since I had just gotten off a ride. We were looking for my mom, not riding the rides and my sister was crying. Once we found her, my parents fought about it, and it was just like every single vacation or interaction with my family. Whatever event it was, it turned into everybody fighting and the passive-aggressive attitudes flying.

I love my parents very, very much. They've saved my ass more times than I can count. I could write an entire additional book about all the times I've gotten arrested, and all the times I've fucked up after they've bailed me out. They FUCKING united when it was time to step up for me.

Despite this, the communication faltered at points. My parents are both a little awkward in small settings but are social butterflies when there are people around. It's an interesting dynamic if you are an observer. If the slightest confrontation or disagreement occurs, the same conversational patterns repeat. My mom will get frustrated and either disengage from the conversation and leave the room (which would cause my dad to throw his hands up and then also leave the room). Or, my mom would get immediately defensive and offer up some type of counterpoint or resistance like: "I was tired."

My dad's pattern is equally as predictable. He communicates quite factually yet roughly in social settings. He doesn't have the most tact. Some examples: he will accidentally say someone looks old or fat or some shit like that. When he says it, it won't be on purpose, but to the people on the other end, it is easy to interpret that it was deliberate. Because of this, then my mom will get defensive and resist. My dad will then make a passive aggressive remark like "I told you so." Then they'd fight and wind up going their own ways for the next couple of days.

I thought that was real life, that everybody's family was the same way. When I went to school, I noticed other people were happy. I wanted to figure out why they were happy, and why the kids that I perceived to be dumb were all in great moods. I kept an eye on what these kids were doing as I got older, so I could emulate what the jocks were doing or what the white trash kids were doing or, what anyone who was happy was doing.

Around 10 or 11, I started playing Dungeons and Dragons and was super nerdy. I got great grades in school and was on a solid path academically. I could do math problems in 15 minutes that would take other people an hour and a half to figure. I was getting 100 percent, A+ answers without using a calculator. I did well in history classes and some of the English classes as well. I could write a great essay in about two or three hours that would take other people weeks to complete.

But I wasn't happy, and at the time, I thought being happy was the most important goal in life. It doesn't matter how smart you are if you're miserable or you're dead, right?

The first time I drank was in Paris on a family vacation. I had a glass of wine with my parents and then ended up sneaking the entire pitcher. That led to dancing with a random 45-year-old lady when I was fifteen. After that, when I got drunk I realized how much fun I had from it, and how much fun the people around me would be having. I thought *this is something I want to do.*

A few months later, I smoked a little bit of pot with a cousin at a family party on Thanksgiving. I didn't really like the taste of alcohol unless it was a sweet wine, but the smoking I could do, even though I had asthma. Suddenly, I was like, "Oh, I'm cool now. I have arrived. I'm gonna keep doing this, and I'm gonna find more people doing this, and I'm gonna make a commitment to changing my life right here, right now."

I was 15, and after that experience, I came back home and shifted my group of friends instantly. I sat at a different table at lunch. I hung with a new group after school and with different people in my classes. Literally, overnight, my grades dropped from As and Bs to Cs and Ds.

I kept up the pace with my drinking and pot for the next couple of years. I went from applying to Penn and the University of Princeton, and all the other Ivy League schools to begging state schools to accept me into their summer session programs. I failed math class senior year and was unable to graduate until my mom dragged the teacher into it and pointed out a technicality on a test. that allowed me to pass the class. As this all went down, I stood there thinking I wasn't going to graduate from high school—and this was after two years of straight A classes and taking honor roll classes, then spiraling into almost becoming a high school dropout.

I got into Bloomsburg, a state school, and attended the summer session.

Throughout it all, I learned that when I decide to do something, I model people around me who I perceive as being successful, and I attach myself to them.

When I saw the burnouts who I thought were having fun, smoking pot behind the tennis courts at lunchtime, sneaking out and hitting a little bowl, I did exactly what they were doing to get into that world. I sold and bought drugs. I participated in the economy of drug dealing as much as I could because that's what it looked like the cool people were doing. As I tell my story, you will notice this is a recurring theme.

Chapter 2: Waterboarding is Definitely Torture

Bloomsburg in the summer is where all the shitty kids go. If you got drunk in high school and had awful grades, Bloomsburg would take you and charge your parents for the opportunity for you to stay there for six weeks and get trashed every single night.

If you've seen *The Wolf of Wall Street*, that's exactly how it was for me, without all the money making. On Monday, we would go to a fraternity party. Tuesday, we would go to a sorority party. Wednesday, I would wake up, start drinking right away, wrap blunts and sneak off, run from the cops, and do crazy shit. Then maybe I would go to class a few times. I ended up getting a bunch of Bs from not going to class, and they put me in honors history courses because I liked history. That whole six-week period was me drinking and having fun every single night, so I thought to myself, *this is how I want my life to be. I want it to be filled with people and relationships and parties and fucking slamming Natty Light.* To take you through a typical frat night (or day), I would wake up around nine or 10, go to class. Maybe, come back from class, get high and start drinking in the dorm rooms. My roommate's name at the time was Ted. We would drink and shit or I would drink with other people, starting around four or five o'clock, and then we would go to a frat party around nine, be the first ones in the door, shake hands with everybody and make friends.

We would get there early so we could have an audience with the people we perceived to be high social status individuals. We'd be in the kitchen crushing beers and shots. By the time midnight rolled around, and the girls started coming out, I'd be throwing up in the backyard or projectile vomiting in the bathroom.

Puking was an almost every night occurrence. Once, I pulled the back of the toilet off and threw up into the tank, so nobody would know that I'd puked in there.

As soon as summer session rolled around, I came into my own with women. I slept with different chicks, pretty much left and right indiscriminately. I hung out and ran from the cops almost every night. I think I got arrested for underage drinking, which will be another recurring theme that you read about.

That party session continued into the next semester at Bloomsburg, where the exact same schedule followed: not going to class, getting drunk, smoking weed, selling drugs.

The next semester, I joined a fraternity. The pledge process was crazy. You see movies about it. You see TV shows. You read articles, but it doesn't do justice to what really happens. Pledging was a five-week extravaganza. They get you a uniform. The first night is called shock night. We lined up in one of the brother's basements. Then the brothers turned a strobe light on and started yelling at everybody. I did probably 50 or 60 push-ups on the spot. They made us run four or five miles to the other end of town. And then back.

There was no drinking yet, nothing like that. After the running, we went home to put on cheap, navy hoodies from Walmart that we were required to wear always when we were "on duty." I don't remember the hours, but they were nuts. You were supposed to go to class and the library. You were supposed to study and get straight As while you were pledging, by the way. But this was not feasible for anybody who was going through the pledge process correctly, so we'd stop going to class because the brothers in the fraternity would keep us at the house until one or two in the morning.

Even if we just had to stay up 'til midnight, we'd have to drink, and they'd throw shit at us, or make us do push-ups and clean. So, we're not getting any sleep, and then we had to be back in the house at noon because they took our class schedules and would expect us to be there at certain times of the day. That was the first week.

When the second week came around, it got a little crazier. There was a lot of memorization. We were required a couple of times a week to recite the Greek alphabet and the names and pledge classes of every single pledge class that had ever come through the fraternity. Instead of studying or learning in classes, I was learning facts about the ancient founding of the fraternity and answers to quizzes that were fraternity-related and had no direct correlation to school whatsoever.

Intermittently throughout this time, everybody had to get drunk at night, all while the brothers threw shit at us and then made us clean it up. At this point, I wasn't showering very often or cleaning my clothes, so I started to smell pretty bad. The same thing happened the next week and the one after that. It was four weeks of being pushed to your limit in a variety of different ways.

22

Hell Week was an entirely different experience. The brothers used super cold water on us, and it was so freezing because the college was in a very mountainous, very northern town, where the weather was brutal.

The running water was maybe 30 degrees. I don't know if you've ever been in 30-degree water, but it is cold. I mean, your bones will ache. We would sit under a spigot, and the brothers would turn it on low flow, and they'd let the cold water run down your back or your head for five minutes. That comprised the first few nights of Hell Week. It would be, you, going about your business and then ice water tossed on you.

And of course, more push-ups.

One time, they filled up a large trash can with ice water that I had to climb into, squat down, and sit in for a few minutes.

Then there was waterboarding. This is different than water torture, which is what they called the cold water. Waterboarding simulates a feeling of drowning. You put somebody upside down, on a slanted table, and you pour water over their nose and mouth, so it makes them feel like they're drowning even though you can't take water into your lungs.

They would pour a gallon on your face and then laugh when you started choking. It's ice cold water, so it sucked even more. The worst water torture was when someone would pull your hood over your face, or put a washcloth over your eyes and mouth so you couldn't see it was coming. It adds a level of fear and horror to that whole experience. Hell Week goes on for five or six days, and then just like that, you're in!

All the torture stops; you start partying, and you become a part of the gang. At this point, I hadn't been going to class for six weeks and was developing a serious drinking problem. My hands would shake from not drinking in the morning.

I'd wake up not knowing what was going on. I thought I was sick or having a seizure, but I really wanted to get a beer, and I didn't know that I was going through alcohol withdrawal until recently. That was my first whole year, so I obviously failed out of school.

For the rest of the semester, I basically sucked down cough syrup and dated chicks. When I'd chug syrup, the girls would wonder why I was going nuts or why I was acting loopy. In reality, it was because I was drinking half a bottle of cough syrup a couple of times a week and then smoking mad weed and drinking like a fish, in addition to selling drugs occasionally.

My level of personal hygiene and care was nonexistent. I'm not brushing my teeth. I'm not showering. I'm not doing my laundry or anything like that. I'm scraping by. I couldn't see it at the time, but other people could. I was the definition of a hot mess before the definition trended.

I also had a lot of random drunken encounters with women. I don't remember 90 percent of their names or what happened during the hookups, but I know they happened, and I thank God, I got out of there without having any kids.

That summer, I went home and hung at my mom's. Then I moved into an apartment with my boy Jayz and my boy Bruh, who were friends of mine from home. Since I wasn't going to school, I had to find a job. Jayz wasn't going to school, so he had to find a job, too, and Bruh got a job at a pizza shop.

To paint a gruesome picture of this phase of my life, let me ask you a couple of questions. Have you ever woken up with blood on your clothing and you weren't sure whose it was? What about vomit? That shit's worse than blood. At least blood doesn't smell that bad.

Chapter 3: If I Don't Remember, Did It Happen?

As soon as I got a job as a telemarketer, I felt like I had arrived. I wasn't going to school. I wasn't being held down by a class schedule. I could do my thing, sell and smoke a little pot, drink and just be free.

I made $9 an hour plus commission at my telemarketer job. I would get people a tune-up for their heating and cooling system, their HVAC. I went through training, and then they stuck me on the phone. In the first hour, I made four sales. That was pretty good since the average rep was lucky to make two or three sales.

Immediately, I felt like *I'm good at this.* Let's crank some loot. So, I'm clocking and closing 10 sales a day. Knocking it out of the park consistently, and more than 20 or 30 percent better than every single other person in there.

I knew I was hot shit and I ate like it, too. After I got my meals next door at the Dollar Tree, I would crush cheese curls and beef jerky, and drink a ton of soda every single day. I was smoking cigarettes, taking Adderall and smoking pot on my breaks. Of course, I was drinking sometimes, too, and living it up.

The game I would spit on the phone was legendary. I would open with: "Hi, Mary?" spoken in a high-pitched friendly tone. When I did this, the person on the other end of the line would think I was an old friend or a local. It's all about tonality, especially on the phone. Mind you; I had NO sales experience then. It was all instincts. I would empathize with people's problems and mimic what I thought their facial expression looked like as they talked to me. Whatever people would say, I would ALWAYS ask for the sale. "Look, either way, you're going to get your heater looked at. Isn't it better to do it now while it's on sale and you don't have to wait for an appointment? You know, they're saying it's getting colder."

That heyday didn't last long. My employer stopped giving me my commission checks because I was always late to work. It was winter and extremely cold. I would wake up at seven or eight o'clock in the morning and walk maybe two and a half miles to work unless Jayz would give me a ride. It was about 20 degrees on that walk and snowed a lot. I would always trudge in late. After too many instances of missing my start time, my company wouldn't pay commissions for a whole pay period; sometimes they wouldn't pay for an entire month. It made me feel like they didn't give a single fuck about me or anyone else who worked for them. The more this happened, the more it became clear that my talents weren't valued.

I only ever got one commission check, which was $500. To clarify, we made a dollar for every sale. I felt like, "These guys are screwing me over." I looked at what they were doing, controlling me and my time, and realized they were not putting me in a position to succeed. In my mind, I was performing well, and they were looking for reasons to not pay me and screw me over, instead of looking for ways to empower me.

While I was there, I traded somebody some of my Adderall, that was prescribed, for Xanax, and of course, I loved it. Xanax makes you feel like nothing in the world is going on, like you're on a cloud and it also makes you black out. So, I would take a Xanax and blink and then it felt like the work day was over, which is exactly what I wanted. I went to my doctor and got a gigantic script of Xanax. It's easy to do because prescription drugs are a widespread problem.

I was taking an ass-load of Xanax, and not remembering anything about my life. I shacked up with a super nice girl, Hanna when my lease was up with Jayz and Bruh. Those guys didn't have their shit together at the time either, although they had the best intentions in the world. When they got bored, they would mess with me. They'd put bologna under my bed, and it would dry out, rot and smell. They would throw broken glass in my room sometimes.

One day, I had only a couple of pieces of clothing. Everything else was covered in broken glass, bad milk, old beer, or printer ink. Ah, that was an absolute shit show. We would drink every single night. We would kill a case every day, or two. And we would all throw in to drink, but then they would fuck with me.

Jayz tried to light me on fire once. A few times they trapped me in the bathroom and poured chemicals under the door. To this day, I don't know why I put up with that. I think it was because I was so weak back then. I moved out of there as soon as I could and moved in with Hanna. It was great for a little while. And then we went to a banquet for the fraternity's big ol' party one evening.

I was taking Xanax and drinking, and Hanna wanted me to quit those things because she could tell how horrible it was for me and I was turning into a monster every time I would use. During the party, I told her I was sober when I was covertly sneaking drinks, filling them back up with water, and then eating Xanax behind her back.

At the party, I said, "Hey, Rachel, I love you." But her name was Hanna. She didn't like that, so she slapped me in the face. She also thought I was nailing her friend, Rox, even though I wasn't. For the next few months, she suspected I was cheating. The reasons? I started waking up too early in the morning, brushing my teeth and wearing cologne, and Hanna would think I was stepping out on her because I was wearing cologne. Because I was brushing my teeth. She would add up everything I was doing in her mind and conclude I was cheating, even though I wasn't. I just had a drug problem.

On top of her believing I had strayed, I lost my job for faking sales, because I was mad, and I was also a dumbass kid.

It was one of the first times everything fell apart, but it wasn't the last.

Hanna rolled out, and suddenly, I was living alone in our apartment, unemployed. I got fat because I was drinking Mountain Dew and eating ice cream and Xanax all day. She hated me.

Fast-forward to the time I sent a letter to the Maury Povich Show asking, "Can we get a lie detector test to prove that I'm not cheating?" Three days later, I was strapped into a polygraph machine, with a camera in my face and BAM, I'm on national television on the *Maury Show* proving to everybody I wasn't cheating on Hanna (yes, we were still going out). Of course, if something like that pops up, your relationship might not be that great in the first place.

I knew we were really going to the show when Hanna got a call and ran into the next room to talk on the phone, which she NEVER did. She came back after she hung up and said, "That was a producer." I was like: "HOLY FUCKING SHIT. THERE'S NO FUCKING WAY. HOLY FUCK." But what I probably said was more like: "Oh, was it?" as if I were all restrained. The producers called us again and then got on the phone with me and asked, "Are you cheating on this girl?" I said, "Nope," thinking all the while *who fucking cops to cheating on the phone with a stranger*? I legit wasn't screwing anyone else, but still? That's comparable to what happens when a cop asks if you're drunk. You NEVER say yes.

After a couple of calls, the producers must have assumed that we were just a couple of fucked up kids because we were scheduled on the show immediately. They said they were filming on Thursday and it was Tuesday. So, the next morning at 5:00 AM, we got into a car and drove all the way to the nearest train station, that was an hour and a half away. We jumped on the train and reached Otto, Connecticut where they were filming at 8:00 AM. I was hungry as shit and toyed with trying the cold pizza with the weird toppings they had put out, but couldn't bring myself to take a bite.

While Hanna was taping the beginning montage, where they tell the backstory, they popped me into a little room with a slutty blonde chick. When I say slutty, picture the worst stripper outfit. Slim cut top, Short shorts more like panties, big hair, big tits, the whole nine. Her makeup was all done up.

This chick's appearance was quite the contrast to mine. I hadn't had a haircut in weeks and was the fattest I had ever been—about 190 pounds. I looked like shit, and I didn't feel the greatest about myself because I worked at Walmart. I was not exactly a desirable male. STILL, she confided in me that she HAD CHEATED on her boyfriend and she thought I was cute. BUT I watched the *Maury Show* all the time and knew it was the "stripper set-up." *There had to be hidden cameras everywhere*. I refused to talk anymore to her once I figured out her intention. Instead, I shut her out, sat back and waited until the next part of my journey with the show.

Twenty minutes later, I'm strapped to a polygraph machine, and the dude running the thing is prepping me. As he got the process going, he casually mentioned that Xanax and benzos would cause the polygraph not to work. I had been out of my scripts for a week and was half-withdrawing, so I was more worried about being a spaz and causing a false positive on the test.

He asked a bunch of baseline questions, like what day was it and then asked a million fucking questions about our situation.

The next morning, extra early, we woke up and went to the studio to do the filming. I was put in a green room with two other guys, both as weird as shit. One of them was from Cleveland and had bought a bunch of Hurricane beer and ecstasy the night before and was still sort of fucked up. He was the first to go out and apparently; they LOVEEEEDDD him on camera. Every couple of minutes, the producers would come in and attempt to coach us on how to act. They would advise that we should be passionate, and they would play with our minds and remind us why we were mad, or why our girlfriends were mad. Clearly, they wanted powerful on-camera reactions.

The other dude in there with us was from Tennessee or Kentucky and had four teeth. Seriously four. He'd gotten caught bangin' hookers on the lie detector test, and was bangin' someone else's cousin, too. The lie detector busted him. I thought it was funny.

Then it was my turn to "walkout" on stage, and it was JUST LIKE YOU SEE ON TV. Every single person in the audience screamed and booed at me. Hanna had already told her part of the story, so I was the bad guy. They asked me if I had a drinking problem and I lied and said I had been sober for nine months. Everyone clapped for me. Then they read the lie detector results, and everyone clapped for me again. Hanna and I hugged and kissed for a second.

It was anticlimactic after such a huge buildup. I had thought that our appearance on the show was going to fix our relationship, so we would be happy again. And it felt that way for a minute. It gave me slight relief as if I could see light on the other side.

Hanna thought I was cheating on her again within a couple of weeks, and we broke up, and I moved back in with my mom. I also tried to detox myself from Xanax, which, I later found out was life-threatening. I had a couple of seizures no one knew about. The withdrawal was bad. Xanax stops you from having emotions, so when you quit taking it, and your emotions come back, you're an absolute monster.

For instance, we would watch a scary movie, and I would be terrified. We would watch an action movie, and I would be sad people were getting killed. My emotions would be over the top, and I would cry so hard. I was super tuned in to people falling in love in romantic comedies. It was so crazy. I also couldn't sleep and could barely eat. I was horribly achy. It was agony. I would not recommend that experience to anybody.

So, I started eating Xanax and drinking again within a couple of weeks. I bought a bottle of Jameson, and I sucked down almost the entire thing one night while I was hanging with my buddies.

My situation at the time was that I couldn't find a job, and I also didn't have a driver's license.

I sold my prescription pills to make money, and I kept doing dumb shit like getting fucking arrested all the time for disorderly conduct or underage drinking. At the very least, I would get pulled over and stopped by the police. But I would do my damnedest to talk my way out of a citation one way or another. This routine went on for a while until I had to get my wisdom teeth pulled and was given a prescription for Percocet.

Then a whole other level of hell hit my life.

Chapter 4: I Fucking Love Percocet

I fucking loved Percocet. I sold a few. I ate a ton of them in a short period of time. You're supposed to take one or two a day. I was taking six or eight a day. A prescription of 30 ran out quickly, so I went from picking my pills up at the pharmacy to buying them on the street. A Percocet can cost $5 or $20, depending on how powerful it is. I didn't have a job. The lack of funds kept my drug problem in check momentarily.

The problem with opiates is it drives your tolerance up quickly. You experience a physical drive to do more; the pain makes you want to keep using drugs, too.

I got a job at my buddy Pho's airbrush studio, managed that for a few years and the fresh stream of money coming in took my drug problem to a whole new level.

I was earning enough money, about $10 an hour, so I could still use and get high when I wanted. Within about a month, I went from taking Percocet to Oxycontin. And I had a drug buddy, too. Shawn was a good friend of mine when we were kids. So, I kind of trusted him, and he was living large in the drug game. He was always worse off than me, doing more coke than I used to do back when I would only do coke occasionally. He was my connection.

I was hanging with Shawn and doing pills all the time. I was snorting Oxycontin, which is potently nuts. To give you an idea of how much that costs, an Oxycontin 80 pill (aka 80 milligrams of Oxycontin) costs anywhere from 60 to 80 dollars. Remember, I was making $10 an hour and smoking a pack of cigarettes a day, drinking a quarter of a bottle of whiskey a day, and smoking pot, as well. I couldn't afford the habit once it got bad and I needed only one a day. The ramp up to that stage of pill insanity was about six weeks.

As all this was happening, I went back to a local community college where I took Sociology, a class I really got into. One day, I was working on a report for class about heroin. I was hanging out with my boy Shawn, who had just started doing heroin only a few days before. So, I said, "Hey, man. Can I interview you about being a heroin addict and what it does?" He replied, "Sure, come on over." So, I went over to his house, and I said, "Do some heroin while I'm doing a report about it for school." He snorted a line. I snorted about 20 percent of the bag, and it made me feel I had done half of one of those $80 pills. A bag of heroin's $10.

You can understand where my thought process went.

Afterward, I was like, "Oh fuck, I'm getting ripped off buying Oxycontin. I'm gonna start buying heroin." So, I went home, and the next day I Googled "where to buy heroin in Philadelphia."

Chapter 5: Where to Buy Heroin in Philadelphia

As I'm writing this book, I am learning a fact about myself. Once I set my mind to a goal, I'm gonna get it, and I'm gonna do it, and I'm gonna perform it at a high level. Unfortunately, at the time, my goal was to be a better drug addict, so I drove up to Kensington, and bought heroin at a street corner, across from two Puerto Rican dudes named Jems and Dabs. Everyone's got an "s" at the end of their name, apparently, up here in North Philly. *Look at me*, I thought as all this went down, *I'm this little suburban white dude in a beat-up Ford Taurus, buying dope on the street*. In that moment, it was also totally normal. Everyone knew why I was there, and the rush of buying it was totally indescribable. It felt like I was getting away with murder every time I went out to get it. And I was doing heroin a couple of times a day.

Two months into my newfound habit of getting high, I bought bags off this dude, Jems.

Because I had found Jems and heroin in Philly from the Interwebs, I learned the Internet could be used to find out a lot of different things. You simply had to be open about how you wanted to find them, and the Internet would deliver. I was driving around in North Philly, or Norf Philly, as the locals call it, just a white boy in a shitty car.

As I'm prowling the streets, this Puerto Rican cat flags me down and says, "Yo, Bud." He waved at my car. When you're in the hood and people try to keep constant eye contact with you it means they're trying to sell you drugs. They will nod and give you a signal that they are a purveyor of fine narcotics.

That's how I met Jems. We exchanged numbers, and I got bags called super-nitro. I fuckin' loved them. Man, they were like fire.

When you start doing dope, at first, it's all good because one bag will get you high all day.

The turnaround is astounding. The next day, you need two bags, and the day after that, you need three or four and so on and so forth until you cap around 10, 20 or 30, or however many you must have to support your habit and can afford. I required five or six bags of heroin over the course of a day to prevent myself from getting sick. My ideal was around 10 or 15. Then I ran out of money, and I didn't know what to do, so for whatever reason that made sense at the time, I managed to get my hands on a gun.

I didn't even know if it was a real gun, but I scratched off all the serial numbers. Then I called up Jems, and said, "Yo, man, I got something for you. Let's make a deal."

I threw that jawn (Philly slang for "thing") in my trunk with my laptop and some *Dungeons and Dragons* books in case I got pulled over.

Jems and I met up and went to get his brother. I was going to get four bundles and some coke for the gun. Jems kept putting off the coke, saying he had to drive and get it, we just had to meet the guy.

As we drove around, the two of them played with my knives. I always carried a bunch of knives, and everybody knew it. We stopped and parked suddenly, and both Jems and his brother pulled the knives on me and said, "Motherfucker, gimme that gat, and you're leaving."

I said, "Shit, if you had just hooked me up with a couple of bundles, I would have made a deal with you." As soon as the words were out of my mouth, his brother starts punching me in the face with the knife handle. I'm like, "Chill, dude! Bro, alright, alright." That was enough to stop them from slamming the handles in my face, and they grabbed the car keys and gun.

I said, "Lemme get my keys back. Don't leave me stranded in North Philly." This happened before Uber. I didn't even have a smartphone.

They threw my keys back to me, and I went home without my dope. The whole incident made me withdraw. I drank some cough syrup to keep an even keel. That's the madness of addiction. A couple of days later, a bold Jems hit me up and said, "George, man. I got what you wanted. You coming down again?"

Of course, I said, "Bro, you just kinda stole from me. I don't know if I could cop dope off you." He told me "Man, I'll give you a free bag or two."

Bam, there I was buying dope off the same dude who'd ripped me off for a couple of bags. It was another one of those times where I knew "Shit. I think I got a problem."

But I still didn't do anything about it.

I learned from that situation, though. An addict will do whatever it takes to get high. I was willing to go to tremendous lengths to keep using drugs. The other life lesson I observed is you can't fucking trust drug dealers. Those motherfuckers do not have your best interests at heart.

Besides, those super nitro-bags stopped being as good anyway. I continued to cop off Jems for a little while after that, driving up to North Philly, meeting him in the middle of the night. I did dumbass shit all the fucking time to get high. Shit that could have gotten me killed way too often.

Once I met this dude who was walking around the street. He was like, "Man, what's good?" I struck up a conversation. Turned out he had some gang connections, and I started buying pills from him. The pills weren't doing it for me anymore, but I bought them to sell to other people, and I kept it up for a while, until one day, when we were in a Starbucks talking, and suddenly, he called me into the corner, and said, "Hey, come close." Then he grabbed me by the neck, pushed me into the wall in the crowded coffee shop, pulled a gun out of his jacket and jammed it in my neck.

I saw the gun as it came near me. It was a Walther PPK 380. He whispered into my ear and pulled me in real tight, so nobody else could see that he had the gun. He said, "If you ever tell anybody what my name is or about this, I'll fucking kill you." And then he held it there for a second longer and said, "Any questions?" I said, "Nope. I think we're all good here, bud." He let me down and put the gun back in his pocket. Then we went about doing business as normal, hanging out. Ironically, I didn't feel threatened when we hung out like I had when he'd had a gun in my neck because I knew if he was gonna kill me that he would have done it right then and there. But he wouldn't have done it in a crowded place. I would never have seen it coming if he was going to do it. At that moment, I knew that I was safe, but I also knew that motherfucker meant business.

I stopped doing business with him because that's not the type of guy I want to be involved with. It wasn't then. It's not now.

That was a moment where I realized, *what the hell is going on in my life?* It showed me I was so out of control.

To give you a time track perspective. I was 20 years old. I had a heroin problem, was connected with gangs, and my car kept breaking down. I also had a weird job in an art studio that would go nowhere and only provide the basics.

Looking back, my life was an absolute roller coaster. It was intensely fun and crazy and intensely dangerous and depressing.

That's the opposite of how my life is now. I still ride the roller coaster of life. (The adventure never really goes away.) But the new roller coaster sounds more like "How happy can I be?" "How many people can I help without getting arrested almost every week?"

Today, I'm in a position to help others and guide them.

Chapter 6: Sir, What Are You Doing?

Not too long after I'd had a gun jammed in my neck and then had my own gun stolen, I moved to a small beach town about an hour away from Philadelphia, to try to get clean. I did it because I really didn't know what else to do, and I was hoping that moving would stop me from easily meeting all my shitty friends and driving up to Kensington to buy dope.

I moved into my grandma's little condo; it was a one-bedroom unit, maybe 700 square feet. When I moved, it was summertime, and I was in a super ritzy town down by the shore in New Jersey called Stone Harbor, near Cape May. I lived there, while I slept my way through my funky little job at the airbrush studio.

I drove back and forth to Philly once a day, still buying heroin and then, using it in the condo, so that attempt to put miles between me and Philly didn't work at all. I even tried to go to a methadone clinic once to get clean. I think I might still owe them 150 bucks. Interestingly enough, I had forgotten to bring a toothbrush and a razor down to beach town. I had only packed a few days' worth of clothes and maybe a half a gallon of vodka, some drugs, and some cigarettes.

I needed to get a toothbrush and mouthwash, and I didn't want to pay for it. So, I went to this little five and dime store.

Picture it: I was absolutely wrecked. Trashed. I'd probably drunk a few shots. I know I'd eaten some Xanax and snorted heroin, and probably Suboxone, too, to try to even out. I might have snorted Adderall, which was prescribed. When you break it down, alcohol and heroin are depressants, so are benzodiazepines. The Adderall would stop me from falling asleep while I was walking, as well as it allowed me to remain relatively coherent, so people couldn't always tell I was using.

That's what I thought anyway, or maybe I convinced myself that was the case.

I know now, everyone could probably tell I was fucked up. I re-wore the same yellow t-shirt and cargo shorts every single day, and I brushed my teeth about every two weeks. My eyes were sunken in, and anyone who took one glance at me knew I was in trouble. When I think back to that time in my life, I should have felt guilty about staying in the condo, but I didn't. I only wanted more drugs.

When I went into the five and dime store, my vision was already blurry. I had the spins. I staggered through the pharmacy section where the toothbrushes and razors are, and grabbed a razor and put it in my pocket. Then I grabbed a toothbrush and put that in my pocket, and for some reason, I think I had toothpaste but no toothbrush. I thought to myself; *you know what? My mouth is real dirty right now, so let's do something about it.* Right there in that store, I grabbed a big bottle of Listerine, and as I was standing in plain sight in the aisle, I opened the bottle to take a swig, and rinse my mouth out. But I realized I didn't have anywhere to spit, so I went to another aisle to take care of my problem.

Then I turned like I was going to walk out, trying to be all shady by peeling two dresses apart on a rack and spitting all over one of them. Well, I spun around to see this guy looking at me, and he asked, "What the fuck are you doing, sir?" I said, "Nothing, get out of my way," and tried to run past him. He was stocking shelves and clearly working and ordered, "No, no, no. You stay right there." I said, "No. I'm leaving." Then I rolled out and headed toward home. He followed me and said the cops were on the way. I looked back at him and snapped, "Fuck you, buddy. Peace."

The cops got there in about 45 seconds because, in a swank town, there are cops everywhere to stop the riff-raff from fucking around. The cops asked, "What are you doing?" and I told them, "Yo, dude. I was just meeting my boy Jason around the corner, and he gave me a toothbrush and this razor. I don't know what this guy's talking about." I probably had a knife on me and drugs, too. The manager insisted, "I saw you put those things in your pocket, and I saw you spit fucking mouthwash all over the place." I replied. "Fuck you, dude. You're a liar. I don't know what you got against me."

The cops knew what was up and questioned, "What's wrong with you?" I was all fucked up. My go-to excuse was always, "I'm prescribed Xanax and Adderall. So, there's nothing you can do about it." They asked to see the bottles, so I took them over to my car parked a block away and showed them the prescriptions. They weren't letting me go and told me, "We have to lock you up for fucking stealing all that shit." Off I went to a holding cell for a few hours, and I didn't really know where I was, at first. Then I came to, like, "Shit. I'm in another fucking holding cell." It was probably the sixth or seventh time I'd been in holding over the course of my life. I was only 21, maybe even 20 years old.

I gave the cops all kind of excuses when I was in lock-up. "You all gotta let me go. You can't keep me back here. I got cancer, man. I could die in this holding cell if you don't let me go." I didn't have cancer, and I didn't even realize what I was saying. What I really had to do was go to the bathroom, and in the holding cell, there was no toilet, for some reason. I think I told them I had stomach cancer and that I was gonna die any second, and they should let me go because my grandma would be mad at me for using. They weren't buying any of that shit. So, they charged me with shoplifting. I eventually got out of it due to a first-time offender's probationary program. I paid a fine and bounced, but that was yet another time where I thought of how I was living my life like, *what the fuck?*

Cape May was the scene of many stories, and when you read the next chapter, you'll learn about another one. And this one? It's the craziest one yet.

Chapter 7. You Can't Drive Like That

Dabs, my Cap May drug dealer was Jem' cousin. We had met when I was out on the prowl and exchanged numbers. I didn't trust Jems because he kept fucking trying to rob me. So, his boy, Dabs, who he was getting his shit from anyway, became my primary source. The prices didn't change, but Dabs came down to the beach condo with his fucking uncle. I don't remember his uncle's name, but he did have a teardrop tattoo and was an older, Puerto Rican guy.

They came over at midnight, on a Tuesday, and we're chopping it up. I was slamming shots of E&J brandy, and railing lines of heroin off my fucking laptop, then chasing it down with shots of brandy. I think it was E&J. It's delicious in ginger ale, and it's cheap as fuck, so you can crush it all day for nothing. Also, the bottle was cool.

Anyway, his fucking uncle goes back to Camden or whatever and leaves Dabs with me. I asked, "Yo, bud, do you want to go to a bar?" It was 1:30 in the morning, and I was awake because I'd been doing drugs all day, snorting Adderall and I think I had a Red Bull or some coffee, too. I had stopped drinking for a few hours, and I'd only had a couple of shots, so I knew I wasn't illegal to drive. But I had snorted heroin and Xanax. That's a whole different realm of intoxicant.

When you're putting a lot of your drugs in your body, sometimes you get sick in a snap before you even know it happens. I would throw up almost at the drop of a hat. A few times, I projectile vomited from the driver's seat of my car into the windshield, on the inside, so then I'd have to drive the rest of the way home from wherever I was going with fucking puke all over myself or the windshield.

On this night, we were driving to a bar down in Avalon. If you know the straightaway where Stone Harbor is, it's a long-ass road where you've got to keep it to 25 miles an hour. My brake lights were out, so I would drive around with my hazard lights on and would get pulled over seriously every day by cops as soon as the sun set. They would let me know my lights were out and I'd shoot back, "Yeah, I know, man. I just got pulled over five minutes ago, and they told me the same thing. I'm driving right home, and I'm going to fix it." That worked probably 15 times, maybe even 20. But it wasn't going to do the trick that night.

I was driving down the road, leaning out the driver's seat of my car, projectile throwing up all over the side of my car. Whatever I'd eaten, probably Chinese food or a Sizzli from Wawa, made it smell crazy rank. Dabs was sitting in the passenger seat, and he looked at the disaster and made a face. "What the fuck, dude? What are you doing?"

I said, "Puking, what does it look like?"

We got to the bar five minutes before it closed, and I had a sip of water to rinse my mouth. Dudes at the door didn't even let us in. We were hanging outside and picked up a couple of chicks. We've got the game. "Hey. Hey, baby, you want a ride home?" Laying it on thick. "Yo, baby, you guys want a ride home or some shit?" They were all enthusiastic. "Oh my God, yeah!" But that's not really what they said because they were fucking shit-faced, too. Dabs is 6' 2" and a pretty strong-looking Puerto Rican guy with a bunch of neck and hand tattoos. Then there's me, a 5' 9" skinny white boy. Not exactly looking the part to pick up girls, and these were some nice, classy ladies, probably from the Main Line or New York or somewhere swank like that.

They got into my car, now covered in vomit and wrinkled their noses. "Hey, what's that smell?!" one of them asked. I'm smooth. "I don't know; I might have run over some dog poop." We made it maybe two blocks and then got pulled over because of my fucking lights. The cop yanked me out, took one look at me and laid it on. "What the fuck are you doing? There's throw-up all over the side of your car. Your brake lights are out, and you're obviously intoxicated." "No, I'm not." Denial was my most frequent response. It was my rebuttal during that time in my life.

The cop rolled his eyes to the girls and then back to me. He left my side to talk to them quick, and I assume what they said was, "I don't even know these motherfuckers. They just picked us up for a ride home, so we didn't have to walk." The cops bought their story and told them to scat. "All right, ladies, you guys can go home."

Then it was just me and Dabs, who was scoffing at the whole mess. He ain't got nothing on him. I didn't have nothing on me; I was just all fucked up. The cops did a sobriety test, and I suggested, "Bro, just breathalyze me. I got a prescription for Xanax and Adderall. You can't do shit." He didn't breathalyze me, but he did impound the car, and he did make me walk about 20 fucking blocks back to my crib.

The next morning, I had to go back and get the car. I swung over and picked up Dabs, and we drove back to Philly. The fee for having my car locked up was $80, but other than that, I got out of that scrape, too. When I look back on all my near misses with the law, it's unbelievable how many times I never got arrested.

Chapter 8: Foolproof Note

In one of my encounters with the police, I was coming back to my grandma's condo from some girl's house in North Jersey, and I was almost out of heroin. This girl was kind of into drugs, but she was not nearly as hooked as me. She didn't do heroin. Still, we were up all night using, and then I slept with her and her sister. She doesn't know that I screwed her sister, though, so hopefully, she never reads this book.

I have a hazy memory of what happened because I was so whacked out. I was up at seven in the morning—that's not usually when I'd wake up—but her parents had come home, so it was time for me to leave. I had one bag of dope left, which was not enough to stop me from withdrawing and I was totally out of money. I barely had money for gas.

So, I thought to myself, *stupid people rob pharmacies all the time, and they can get away with it. I'm really smart, so I should be able to do that, no problem,*" which, of course, was sound thinking.

To set the scene, I was wearing filthy dirty, white shell tops, from Adidas, with blue stripes, and beat up jeans. I hadn't showered in a couple days. My hair was long, and I was out of my mind.

I pulled into the pharmacy parking lot, and the only reason I can share this with you is that I, already pled guilty, and got off with probation. These are the facts, but you can read them yourself since the incident is a matter of public record.

When I walked into the pharmacy, I asked, "Do you guys have Dilaudid, Opana?" I added, "My grandma needs a prescription for it." She didn't. The pharmacist shot back, "Yeah, you need a prescription, though." I went with it "Okay, cool." So, I left, got out to the parking lot and fucking swung my whip around the corner. Then I parked a couple of blocks away, so I could change my clothes. Since I'd walked in with a wife beater and jeans, I thought I could pull off a new identity with a jacket, hat, and sunglasses. Then I wrote a note and pulled on a pair of gloves.

The note was brilliant and said something to the effect of "Yo, give me your drugs," and listed out some narcotics. I had also written, "Or else someone's going to kill my family." In my state of lunacy, I thought I could give the guy the note, and it would fix my problems. I was confident my fucking criminal mastermind outfit hid the old me. The guy looked at the note and then said, "Okay, man. No big deal. Give me like two minutes. They're locked up in the back."

Instead, he picked up the phone. I saw the three numbers he punched in. Then he said, "Yeah, CVS," and hung up the phone. Immediately, I lashed out, "You mother... You fucking called the cops. What the fuck?" But the whole time I was thinking, *what am I doing? Has it really come to this? What is happening in my life right now, that me, George Beatty, a nice kid from the fucking suburbs is robbing a pharmacy? Let's get real.*

That was it. I took a deep breath and walked out.

I never saw the pharmacist again. He didn't come outside. I walked away and didn't look back. Just dragged my ass over to my car, jumped in, went to my grandma's house, grabbed my bike and then smoked a cigar. It might have been a blunt, but I needed a hit to calm down because I'd had an immense adrenaline dump. My hands shook.

As I was sitting there, trying to chill out, riding my bike and feeling my nerves settle, I saw a state trooper parked in my grandma's driveway. My eyes got wide. "Fuck." It's those motherfuckers. There's no way they're here for me." They didn't appear to be going anywhere, so I moseyed over to see what was going on.

As soon as I rode my bike onto the driveway, the cops were on me. "Are you George?" I'm like, "Yeah." Meantime, my grandma has the look of fucking death on her face. She's all worried. You could see it. My grandad had Lewy body dementia, so he didn't know the extent of what was going on, but I could see concern on his face as well.

The cop walked toward me gesturing. "Come over here. Can I look in your car?" I think they were checking for the clothes, and I denied him, "Nah, motherfucker. You can't look in the car," and he said all suspiciously, "Well, it looks like you were trying to rob this pharmacy." I shook my head. "I don't know what you're talking about. I was here the whole time. I got home a few hours ago," trying to make an alibi up on the spot.

"Nah, bro. I'm pretty sure this was you. You're wearing the same shoes that were in the video."

"No, I'm not."

Of course, I was, and they were recognizable. Fucking Adidas shell tops. Everybody had those shoes. At least, it seemed everybody had those shoes because you know when you have something, you see other people with it all the time.

My lawyer, who had handled my shoplifting case, was going to handle this one, too. I called him and said, "These cats want to look in my car. Should I let them?" My lawyer wanted to know if they would find anything that could incriminate me, and I told him they would, and he said, "Then you shouldn't let them fucking look in the car." Apparently, they needed a warrant. While all this was going on, my mind was spinning, and I was trying to figure out how they knew it was me. I'm guessing they had checked the cameras, to see my car from when I had gone in there to ask if they had any drugs. Maybe I had gotten a speeding ticket, or a parking ticket, or a citation? Then I recalled the night with Dabs' and how I had picked up a ticket for driving without my headlights.

The cops had cross-referenced the address since I had given them my grandmother's address when I got the ticket. Then they had shown up. I also had a couple of pounds of fake weed in the car. You know that fucking Old Spice shit. It's sort of illegal, but not really. So, I, 100 percent didn't want them searching the car.

Time went by as we stood there talking to the cops, while they did the *Law & Order*, good cop, bad cop routine. Finally, the one cop said, "Look, bud. You got to get in the back of this cop car."

"The fuck I do."

In a hot second, I was handcuffed and stuck in the back of the car. I was still fucked up and half in another dimension because of the other cocktail of drugs I'd taken. Again, my grasp of the truth is fuzzy, but I kind of remember drinking that morning, and I do remember taking Xanax and Adderall, to deal with my heroin withdrawal.

For the millionth time, I was shoved into a holding cell for several hours. It was the perfect time to pass the fuck out. Since I was leaning over and trying to sleep while I had the cuffs on, I ended up getting cuts on my wrists, and I still have the scars.

When I woke up, my mom was standing in front of me. She lived a couple of hours away and had come all the way down to pick me up, but they'd never fingerprinted me. They never did shit. They just let me go, and I had no idea why for the longest time, until recently. But hang in there with me, because there is an ending to that story.

I went back to my mom's place for a few days, then got into a car accident and totaled my car. It kind of wasn't my fault, but it kind of was. A guy swerved into my lane, and I spun. I'm pretty sure I was smoking weed in the car and that I was all fucked up. My car was totaled. I had just gotten arrested.

My life had devolved into absolute madness.

A few nights before my accident, I had been hanging at Dabs' house. Literally, I had gone to my drug dealer's actual place of residence. We railed lines of dope. It was my 22nd birthday.

Chapter 9: Whatever It Takes

When you're using and especially, when you're low on money, you will do whatever it takes to keep getting high. Everybody falls to different bottoms when they're using; everybody ends up doing different, odd shit when they're using. I was stealing money from my mom, my dad, and even my grandmother. Whoever I could get money off to go use one more time. Besides the job I had, which was just me falling asleep in my chair every day, and the pills, and the drinking, I was stealing from some of my friends, too. I tried to steal five or 10 dollars when I could. Then I would drive off and get high with it.

Almost every day was an insane struggle to use just one more time. The pain defies explanation when you stop. At some points, I would say to myself; *I don't want to use anymore. I don't want to do drugs anymore. I just want to be normal. I'm not going to do heroin anymore.* Then suddenly, I'd find myself driving out by I-95 North to get another bag. Within a week, literally every time I was in my car, I would say to myself, "I want to stop this, and I don't know how. God, help me, please help me." I would cry because I couldn't turn the car around and I would slam my fist on the steering wheel because I didn't know what to do. It hurt so bad. I don't ever want to go back there.

Every time I think about it, I get goosebumps realizing where I am now, and where I was then. Actually, as I'm writing this today, it's my six-year clean date. So, this day has an extra special meaning to me. I can still remember the pain vividly even though it's been so long. I hope that agony never happens to you or any of your family members. The reality is, most people aren't able to get out of that vicious cycle, and they die. I've had 50; maybe even 80 friends die since I've gotten clean. It's indescribable torment knowing it's all preventable.

Let me take you back in time before the car accident, so you can understand how desperate I was and how that accident would change my life.

I started running a little money because I *had to* since I'd lost my job when the customers stopped coming in. My habit had gotten up to about a bundle of dope a day, which is 10 to 15 bags, or 100 dollars a day. That amount is what it cost me to get high, which, again, was unsustainable based upon the number of hours I was working, and despite my stealing.

Because I had no money, those times when I had to stop, were cold turkey, with a few drugs thrown in to ease my withdrawal.

Before the shop closed and on the day of my accident, that led to the biggest and best change in my life, I drove up to work to collect my paycheck early. I needed to use, but I got into that car accident, and that was the catalyst for change.

After the crash (and because of it), my mom thought I had a behavioral problem, not a heroin problem. So, she took me to outpatient therapy to help me get straight in the head and kick my suspected pot habit. The counselor's name was Ken Williams. And I've got to say, man; Ken saved my fucking life.

When you think of drug counseling, you envision a fucking boot camp. Someone yelling at you and beating into you what you need to do to get clean all day. Ken wasn't like that at all. I would sit in his office for an hour, and we would talk. Just make friends. Our time didn't even cover drugs at first.

Ken was an old biker guy who had been clean for a long-ass time. His easy demeanor put me at ease, and I loved our vibe.

Ken and I would bust it and right off the bat; he treated me like I was a regular person and not a patient. He made a point to say he was on my side and not my parents' side. I figure he had picked up on the sometimes-turbulent relationship I had with my family.

We shared, "This is who I am. This is who you are. How do you feel about gangs in New York during the 1970s?" We talked about the Westies in Hell's Kitchen, and other cool topics.

Ken had wild, white hair and a scruffy beard. You could see the pits in his face, probably from scratching at make-believe meth bugs. When you do meth, some people like to pick at their faces. Ken was an old meth head who had been sober 20 years. His office was a comfy spot. It wasn't that big, but he had a nice couch, a ton of art and his dog, a cute little schnauzer named Serenity.

My mom told Ken what happened in her words, and I told him, too. I remember distinctly the conversation we had. To clarify, I was out of money. I was out of drugs. I had gotten in a car accident and totaled my car a day or two before. I was car-less. Broke. Drugless.

I'd found some cough syrup that had been in my mom's house. It was way back in the linen closet and had been there for 10 years. My new habit was hitting about a half a bottle because I was withdrawing from heroin. I was a little fucked up, to put it mildly. Also, if you guys have drugs in your medicine cabinet that are years old, throw them away, because your kids might take them.

Ken said, "What the fuck happened with you getting arrested and getting into fights and shit?" I told him, "I don't know, man."

After two minutes and two seconds, I lost my grip. "Bro, that wasn't even me!" Spinning some story. Ken knew the truth, and then I slipped and told him I had tried heroin for the first time, even though I was a full-blown heroin addict.

It was a cry for help. Ken fucking put his pencil down, took off his glasses off, and said, "What?"

I shrugged. "It's no big deal. My buddy had a little dope, and I snorted some of it."

He said, "Did you use a needle?" I told him no.

That's when he stopped fucking around. "Someone I know who was clean for five years and just went out for a quick one fucking died yesterday. You're going to rehab."

"No, I'm fucking not going to rehab!"

"You're going to rehab."

Then I thought about it, and said, "If I'm going to go, now is the time. I'm out of money. My mom's about to kick me out, I just crashed my car again. It's time."

"It'll be just like summer camp," he tried to reassure me. "You stay overnight. They feed you. You play games all day. And ta-da!" That was supposed to be the day-to-day.

I went deep inside, doing the math in my head, with what was going on in my life. When I came up for air, I knew the truth. "I do want to get clean!" I remembered sitting in my car crying because I couldn't turn the car around on the way to North Philly, slamming my fist on the steering wheel. It hurt inside and out.

I was out of money. I was out of drugs. I was facing a serious, serious criminal charge. I had to go to rehab. So, I told him to call. He rang up a local rehab, and because it was right in the middle of the heroin epidemic, of course, they didn't have any beds open. They wouldn't have a bed for 72 hours. I had to fucking white-knuckle it until then.

Segue to me detoxing on my mom's couch in the living room. Trying to sip that bottle of cough syrup, the one I didn't tell anyone about, and that allowed me to not get too deadly ill. I spent the next few days crying. My dad bought me a pack of cigarettes for the first time in his life.

As I was laying in my hellish state, I got honest about how I fucking needed that smoke more than I needed air.

"Look, Dad. I smoke cigarettes, and I'm fucking out of money. I don't want to sell drugs. I don't want to do anything anymore to get drugs. I'm tired, but I really do need a cigarette. I'm trying to stop doing heroin."

Just like that: "I'll fucking go buy some." And he did.

A couple of days later, with my tail between my legs, I wore a nice shirt with some sweatpants and tried to fucking impress the rehab people at Mirmont Treatment Center. That walk in the door and to the admitting area was tough.

Right there, right fucking then, I made the decision to turn my life around. If I was going to go to rehab, I was going to fucking do it, and I was going to go all in. I was going to get clean and change my life. Because there was not another second that I wanted to spend using drugs.

Chapter 10: Getting Clean

The very next day I fucking wake up, and I'm in a detox. For those of you who haven't been in a detox before, it's set up just like a college dormitory. I had a roommate, a bed, dresser, no sharp objects. You weren't allowed to have a razor or any mouthwash because there's alcohol in mouthwash. You couldn't have hand sanitizer. The staff searches all your shit to make sure you're not smuggling in a needle or dope, and then they give you Suboxone to detox. I personally did not take any Suboxone when I was in, but a lot of other people did.

They drug test you to see what you have in your system, and then you fucking just detox. It's almost like you see it in the movies. But you have to wait until it's over. It's a grueling ride, and they try to make it as cool, calm and comfortable as possible. You have the same goal, to just hang on and get through it.

You meet a ton of people in rehab and one of the things they tell you is, "Stick with the winners. Stick with people that want to stay clean. Stick with people doing the right thing and getting clean, who are not getting into trouble and not using drugs." If you can believe it, there are a lot of people getting high in rehab. I learned real quick that the type of person I wanted to be around was somebody I wanted to model my life after—someone serious about getting clean and who had reasons for doing it. They had made the decision to change. They were fucking rocking toward it. They weren't stealing food, cigarettes, and money because that kind of shit happens in those sorts of places.

Fake gangsters. Real gangsters. Kids from the mainline. All the rich kids, and a mix of everyone in between. It's a combination of people, and because of that, it feels like you're in high school, even though it truly is like summer camp. Once you get out of detox, you have to attend small group counseling sessions, where you and everybody else fucking fight through the issues, and talk about relationship problems with parents, and why you think that you get high.

I ended up being in rehab for only 17 days. My insurance booted me out after that. One thing they don't tell you about rehab is they don't send you for 30 days. They only send you for as long as your rehab will pay, which is a revolving insurance issue. It's almost exactly like a pill mill—and it's one of the reasons I found drugs while I was in rehab.

Chapter 11: Surviving Rehab

The only exposure I had for what rehab was going to be like was from TV, and I made a point not to watch shows like *Intervention* because it hit a little close to home for me.

I didn't know what to expect. When I was 17, a friend of mine went to rehab, and when he came out, he started using immediately. So, you can understand my original impression of rehab was as if it was some type of brainwashing zone like you would see in a re-education camp in Russia.

I made it, in part because of Ken. He coached me through making that very tough decision to fucking go into rehab and admit that I had a drug problem. What sold me was the way he described the daily regimen.

You wake up at six or seven, have breakfast and a couple cigarettes. Then you go to a meeting or a group class with the whole rehab population. You say hi, and you do this, and you do that, do this, do that. Simple.

A couple of people would share how they felt the night before, whether they'd prayed. They're very heavy on the

God thing and the 12 steps. If you guys have ever encountered any literature regarding Alcoholic Anonymous or Narcotics Anonymous, you'll see a lot of references to the 12 steps, which they lean on in rehab.

You go to the morning class, do some hoo-rah stuff to get pumped, and then you get a break. Typically, there's meditation or yoga during the day, or you can work out, but you will take part in an exercise that is designed to incite mindfulness. Mindfulness is super effective for treating addiction.

Then you have lunch, and after lunch, you do small group therapy. A lot of the core therapy people think of when they envision rehab happens in those small groups. The small group consists of you, a counselor, and between five and eight other people. It's more of an intimate setting. You share where you're at, what happened with you, why you're at rehab, and then you get into other topics, and everything you experience, hear, or share has varying levels of severity. People came from all kinds of different backgrounds.

One of the people in my small group at the time, I don't remember his name, was from Puerto Rico. The Puerto

Ricans round up all their drug addicts and tell them they're sending them to rehab, or they're sending them to get help. Then they drop them off in North Philly, which is where all the drugs get sold. This had happened to the guy who was speaking, but then he had gotten a job and health insurance, which is why he could go to rehab.

Some other guy was stalking his ex-wife still. Another lady had a bunch of other problems. It was a circle where people would talk about their issues. Immediately, as I sat there and listened, I thought, *oh, fuck. It's not that bad for me. Could be way worse.*

I connected with my counselor because we both had an interest in the Civil War. We bullshitted a bit. I made temporary friends.

It did turn out to be somewhat like summer camp in some ways. But it other ways it wasn't, like when the counselors try to get you as separated from the drugs as possible. They try to get your mind as far away from those drugs as they can and pull you out of that shit.

By the end of my stint, I knew 100 percent, I could not go home. I couldn't move back in with my mom. I couldn't be around my old friends (if you could call them friends). I needed to be geographically and physically somewhere else if getting clean was going to work and if it was going to stick.

The only thing I wanted was to get clean. I wanted to do something with my life, whether it was working in a fucking factory, or building a business. I knew the life I did not want was the drug life. So, I had to get as far away as I could. That would be the surest bet I could make for myself.

When I mentioned my idea to my counselor, he said, "We're going to send you to Levittown." Levittown, at the time, and probably still is, is the recovery capital of Pennsylvania. That city probably had 100 individual recovery homes, that were run like halfway houses.

He told me who he wanted me to connect with and who would keep me safe. Then he called a gentleman named Brian Kennedy, who fucking took the reins from there and saved my life.

Brian, hey, man, if you're reading this, thank you for doing me a solid. I know we had some rough patches there, but you're the fucking man, and I'm forever grateful.

A few days before I was supposed to check out, it was right after the night meeting wrap up where everybody talks about their day at the alumni meeting. The alumni come back for these meetings, and they are people who have been clean for a little while. The reason they bring them in is to show the people in rehab that the program works. That a clean life is possible.

Brian had gone to the rehab center and had been clean for two or three years. He was the operations manager and director of a larger recovery house, an organization that probably had 10 or 15 locations in Levittown, Pennsylvania.

The general structure of their organization was, you move into a Phase One House, which takes people who are 30 to 60 days clean. After that, they move you to a Phase Two House, where the restrictions are lighter. You're allowed to spend more time with your friends, out of the house and enjoy more leniency. Phase Three is a normal sober house. The only rule of importance in the sober house is that you can't use drugs. You can have girls over. You can stay out late. All the other phases have curfews, and you wouldn't make it to Phase Three until you'd been clean around six months.

I met Brian, who worked for an organization called Life's Journey, and we had a quick conversation about my background, whether I was going to have trouble finding a job, etc. He asked me about my family's history and my history. Then stuck me in the house, named Gooseneck, titled after the street where it was located. Gooseneck would have kids from nicer neighborhoods, which, for me, at the time, was a big deal.

As much as I might've painted the image of myself as a street guy, I'm not. I'm a nice kid from the suburbs in my heart. So, throwing me in a traditional Phase One House would have meant contact and rooming with actual gangsters and goons.

I wouldn't have done very well.

Chapter 12: Life's Journey

Suddenly, I went from living with my mom and sort of almost out of my car to living with like nine or 11 other dudes. I had one single roommate. My first roomie was a guy named Jayce who was pretty cool. He got a job flooring or got placed in another house within a couple of weeks.

Then along came Moe, my next roommate. Moe was a very interesting character. I want you to know; I'm just telling the story here—simply repeating Moe's words. I don't know how much is true or how much isn't true. Moe was an ex-Special Forces guy, who had also joined the French Foreign Legion when he had a drinking problem, and then was a mercenary in Libya after the war broke out. He guarded oil fields, and wouldn't talk about any of that part of his life much. At first, I thought the guy was full of shit. But he had a couple of friends who had known him for a long time who vouched for him. He would do push-ups and run 10 miles along with a lot of other crazy shit. All things considered, he was an alright dude.

No one was jammed into this house. Some recovery houses will have four or five people in a single bedroom. This one had two each in a bedroom, so the place had more of a dorm-room feel. You are put into the house with men of varying ages. I was 22 at the time and the second youngest person. The oldest person was 55 or 60. They had been drinking for 50 years and couldn't get sober.

This was the house Brian Kennedy had lived in for a little while. He had moved out to another house, however. I think he got into an argument and ended up leaving.

Again, our success hinged on routines. We would wake up at 7:00 or 8:00, and then go out on a job search from 9:00 to 5:00, before going to a meeting, like AA or NA. Then you'd come home. When you got home, you would do a chore like cleaning the kitchen or sweeping the steps. Then you would go to bed.

If you're currently struggling with addiction or know somebody who is, I cannot recommend highly enough doing something to continue your treatment after you get out of rehab whether you need to stay in a recovery home or a halfway home. You can even stay in an extended outpatient treatment center somewhere. All the research seems to show that longer treatment results in a higher chance of staying clean.

In a recovery house, you shift roommates all the time, and they constantly move you around. People are either moving on, getting jobs and progressing through life or they're using. Sometimes, they might have to leave because, frankly, they're dying.

It was time for me to get a job. I was on the hunt and was ecstatic to have fucking quit heroin, just super stoked with a new spark for life. Kind of on that pink cloud as they say. I got a job taking surveys in the mall, kicked ass at it and collected mad surveys. It was a sort-of commission position. The manager told me to tone it down because I was too high energy, and too aggressive at getting people to sign up. When that happened, I knew that gig wasn't the right one, plus I was only making eight bucks an hour.

Chapter 13: Selling TVs

Before long, I got another job selling TVs for commission. Everybody in the house was telling me to find a minimum wager, a $10 an hour job somewhere else because commission was unreliable, and they weren't sure I could do it. In my heart, I believed if I just stuck to what people told me to do, everything would work out, and I could pay my rent in the recovery house.

You guys think I'm gonna fuck this up when in my heart I know I can make this work? That's what I would think when people tried to talk me into getting a different job with a more reliable hourly rate. I knew if I just followed whatever system they gave me, I could make at least enough to pay my rent, which was 150 bucks a week. I would also have enough left over to pay for cigarettes and going out.

I took the job, got through the training in a week or two that entailed following around a salesman. The sales training was "Okay, this is a TV. These are the three main things people ask about it. Now go sell them." *Uhhhh...okay?* My manager assured me, "If they like you they'll buy shit from you. Just ask them if they want to buy it." *Alright.*

All I needed to do to get somebody to want to buy from me was find out if it was a good fit for them. If it was, then they would buy it, and if it wasn't, they wouldn't. I figured if I showed enough people enough TVs, that a certain number would buy one. Then I could pay my rent and loosen my belt.

I'd never really lived in a clean setting. So, keeping things up and staying on top of my chores was tough for me. As soon as I got a job, I delegated my chores out and negotiated with people as to how much I wanted to pay them, usually like five to 10 dollars, to scrub the kitchen for me or mop the floor. I did the math in my head of how much it would cost in time, and how much I wanted to do it, and how much I made per hour. I thought to myself; *I average $20 to $30 an hour selling TVs. It takes an hour to do this chore that I don't like doing. Somebody else will do it better.* It was worth it for me to pay a couple bucks and leverage my time.

There are several types of arguments you get into at a halfway house, besides when people come home high or drunk, in which case they get drug tested and thrown out. The most common arguments happened when someone ate someone else's pizza or eggs, whenever someone ate too much of the food or used someone's conditioner or soap. We had constant issues like that, so there was a lot of bickering and fighting over the small stuff. The same three to five problems pop up, and there is endless manipulation, too.

A couple of people relapsed and died a few times, and a few more relapsed and got kicked out. There are, unfortunately, too many of those stories to tell in a book. But it gets awful and sad far too often.

Eventually, I moved from Gooseneck to another one of the houses called Indigo. It was the same story just a different chapter. I was still selling TVs when I transferred to my buddy, Jeremy's sober 7/8 house, (where the only rule is that you can't do drugs—and you WILL be drug tested). It was a definite upgrade but for the same price.

Meanwhile, in my job, I noticed a lot of salespeople in the store were kind of lazy; all they wanted to do was talk to each other and make jokes. Man, I wasn't there to talk. I was there to make money. I was there to get paid. I wasn't there to make friends, and most of those cats just seemed like losers anyway.

I was always on point, which in sales means you're up. The next customer is yours. You had to stand in a certain place to be on point, and no one would ever stand there, so I took that spot. Before I knew it, I started making $800, $900, maybe $1,000 a week, which at the time, felt rich. I went from making $10 an hour and blowing it all on drugs to having real money. To a 22-year-old kid with no college degree, $40,000 a year is a lot of money.

The other salespeople grew to resent me because I was making a lot of sales and because I was getting up off my ass when they had this unspoken system where they all wanted to bullshit as much as possible. Eventually, they would just take the people who were walking in and ready to buy. Not me. I wanted to make sales and do my job. So that's what I did.

Almost overnight, I was the top salesman in the store and one of the best in the region. As a drug addict, I'd never had any disposable income. I knew I could make it somehow in sales without having to go back to college to be a lawyer, engineer, librarian, or an accountant or some other boring profession. In sales, I had a shot. But I still had to hone my craft and get better.

My sales technique wasn't necessarily browbeating people, coercing hard sales or rebuttalling. I wasn't especially great at those methods. What I was especially great at was building rapport and trust in people by putting their needs first and finding out what was best for them. Knowing that over the long run, it would work out for my clients, and therefore, it would work out for me.

As I said to myself and the managers, "I want to get promoted. I want to manage one of the stores and make this a career." And I did want that, but I continued to sell TVs. Deep down I craved the security of making 45 grand a year, which was less than I was making as a salesperson by then, and I was so scared to keep selling. Everyone who was and who I'd talked to about it had told me it was a bad idea and that I was going to fail. But I knew, I KNEW I could do it. Because of the negative environment and everyone trying to snake me, I thought there had to be something better out there. I got passed over for that promotion partially because I was young, and partially because of my history. I had only been clean for six months.

One day, a guy came in and bought a TV from me. He told me he used to sell windows and siding, but he'd since retired.

I liked the guy. He seemed sharp. He had done a lot of business and said, "You know, you can make $100,000 or $150,000 a year." He worked for one of the biggest department stores there was, but selling windows.

"Holy fuck!" $100,000 a year?" He had my attention. *That's rich, like what my mom or dad makes. It's a lot of money. I need to do that.*

The window guy laid it out. "You eat what you kill." Meaning, you make money based on your performance. There's generally a lot of support. There's a lot of autonomy. And you can do it without a college degree.

It seemed like a logical shot.

The guy mentioned in passing that the window place was always hiring and their training was stellar. One question that I always ask when I'm going into a new job is "How is your training?" One asset nobody can ever take from you is an education. One strength nobody can ever take from you is a skill. That's yours forever. I'm always looking to enter an organization to build my mental sharpness, or to sharpen my stick, so to speak.

Turns out a buddy of mine, Andrew, worked for the window place as a canvasser. He went door-to-door making sales and then referred me in. He talked to me about the company and said working for them was the greatest choice he had ever made. The company support was incredible. Management gave a shit about him, which had not been my experience. I had learned management always cared about the bottom line, not about the employee.

Again, he sang their praises. "Last year they took us on a cruise for a fucking company Christmas party."

"What? These motherfuckers took you on a cruise? We didn't even have a party. The closest thing we ever had to a party was Dunkin Donuts coffee, and they didn't even get enough to feed everybody."

I sent them my resume and got a call ASAP. The organization had been around for 20 years and was subtly adjusting their sales program to build it into a science. A science of sales, and a science of getting somebody to buy windows from you. If I went with them, I would be plugged into the system. I would learn their science and their methods to get people to buy.

There's one question that I always ask in a job interview. The lead-in goes like this: "Based upon my qualifications, my resume, and this meeting, can I expect to hear back from you? If so, can I expect to receive a job offer?" In effect what you're doing, especially from a sales perspective, is right there, in the moment, you're asking for the sale, which is the job. You're selling them on giving you the position.

I asked my magic question of the hiring manager, and he looked down at his notes, took a deep breath, and then peered back up at me. "You've got the job." He just fucking gave it to me. In my head: *Oh my God. It worked! I rolled the dice and took that shot, and I got that shit.* I was so excited! *I could make $100,000.* That fuck ton of money to me at the time was all the money in the world, like $2,000 a week. I wasn't even worried I was going to fuck it up. I cannot describe how joyful I was, and how proud of myself I was that I had nailed it and could finally change my life. I knew I had to double down and go for it in a way that nobody else had, and I knew that I had to take full advantage of the opportunity.

I started the job a couple of weeks later. We had an orientation day where the CEO, who I still look up to, held a new sales class. He gave us a little 20-minute talk that covered "This is what we do. This is what we're about."

We went around the room and said why we were there. People explained their reasons they had taken the job, rattling off words like: "The insurance." "The benefits." "The training." "The culture." Then they came to me, and I blurted out, "Man, I really don't know about insurance or any of that stuff. I'm here to make a lot of money." Corey chuckled and said, "At least we've got one honest sales rep here." I obviously chuckled at that, too, because it really was why I was there. It was a good reason for me and a better reason for the company.

Chapter 14: Slingin' Windows

The training for that company was insanely difficult, but on the other side, it was, kind of amazing. I had been clean for six to eight months by then. I was going to a meeting every day, sometimes two in a day, hanging out with the guys in the recovery houses, and I was still getting moved around. Then I was moved into a sober house.

As I was selling the windows and going through the training, I was staying up from six or seven o'clock at night to five in the morning. And I did this every night for two weeks in training while memorizing exactly what to say, how to say it, the mannerisms, every little thing I could learn and do to be successful. It paid off because I hit the ground running, and was the best performing salesperson in my training class. Because of my performance, I was immediately fast-tracked for a leadership position.

When I bagged the window job, I was on fucking cloud nine. I also knew as soon as I got it, that's when the real work would start, and it would be my time to shine. The training for the job lasted four weeks and required the memorization of the sales pitch, which basically entailed: "Do this three-hour long pitch word for word."

I had to learn it and buckle down to get it right, so I listened to the sales manager say it, then recorded it. Then I would listen to it and write it and say it at the same time. If I messed up, even just on one word, I started over. Every single "the" was in the same place, every single emotion or tic was in the same spot, and I would do it until I memorized each sentence.

I cornered my friends and practiced the window pitch. My routine was going to people's houses on prequalified appointments and pitching them on buying new windows. Windows typically cost $300, and the windows I sold were $1,000 a piece, so you had to be prepared when you were selling prospects; it was not a situation where you could just walk into an appointment and wing it.

My employer took their training seriously, so I fucking did it. and I closed two of my first three leads. I was the best one in my class of nine people.

We had a couple dropouts right away—people who couldn't hang and couldn't do the volume. It was a hard job, and you were on duty between 10 AM and 8 PM. If your phone rang with a lead, you were supposed to have two hours to get there, but sometimes you had only 30-45 minutes.

Your phone would ring, and you'd be ready to drop everything, run the lead and get paid. The window joint used a sliding commission scale based upon the margin we sold. Depending on the margin, you'd make 7 percent of the sale price or 12 percent of the sale price.

I followed that process for three years and learned a lot. So much of what they taught was how to relate to people and the foundational bullet points that you always had to hit to make a sale. The first bullet point was to believe that you could make it. If you didn't think you were going to make a sale or that you could help the people you were going to see, you weren't going to do shit. You weren't going to make the sale. You were going to waste your time and their time, so you had to believe in yourself. Then, you needed to build rapport and trust. Let me impart that trust is the most important part of that equation.

If people trust you, they'll believe what you have to say. If you're coming from a genuine place of trying to help them and make sure they don't get ripped off by some fly-by-night contractor, they'll go with you. That's what I did, and that's what I tried to focus on, delivering my pitch well. But I hit a lot of ups and downs. I was put into a leadership group quickly. But because I'd gotten the job when I was only 22, from a maturity standpoint, I wasn't ready to take on a larger role, even though I thought that I was ready. By then, I was consistently making two grand a week. I felt like I had made it, even though they hit you with the old W-2 and the taxes, the health insurance, and all that shit. It didn't matter because, at that time, that gig was bitchin.'

Another thing I picked up at the leadership group, and this is vital to remember, is the way they employed people and the way they structured their business. I've got to fucking hand it to my sales manager. That dude is a straight killer, gangster, one of the best salespeople I've ever met. He and J-Dub, those guys were awesome, and they changed my life by giving me a shot.

I was finally in a place that took care of their employees first, because when you take care of your employees, they'll take care of the clients, and the clients will take care of you. It's a circle of everybody taking care of one another. They threw us parties, did open bars. I quit drinking when I went to rehab, but that was still an effective way of motivating all the employees there.

I was lucky to be in a company that was good at making people feel significant and feeding their self-esteem. They did daily sales shout outs, so whoever did well the night before would get a pat on the back when their accomplishments would be noted in an email.

I got passed over for a promotion, which to this day I suspect was because I don't drink and because of my addiction history. And I'm sure being young and emotionally not ready had a lot to do with it. I had moved for the company, not to a different city, but to be closer to the office, to a not-so-great neighborhood. I wanted to make sure if I got promoted, I could perform. I was on track, too. Everything was falling into place. I had tripled my sales and was on pace to make $150K that year. That's when I learned I really didn't want the management position. I wanted to do more for myself.

But then in July of 2014, I got sick, and my story changed yet again.

Chapter 15: Kayla

I wouldn't be doing this book justice without talking about my ex-girlfriend, Kayla, who I started dating when I was just getting clean and who stayed with me up until the time I first landed in the hospital for my mysterious illness. I met her online after I'd been clean for about a year. I fell in love with this girl so fast and so hard. Right from the moment I met her. There was just something about her that made me want to be around her more. She had moved to the area where I was living on a whim, and at that point, I was still in the sober house. Her family was no good, so she left California and ran to Pennsylvania about a year before we met. She seemed to have a bit of a troubled past, which I could really relate to.

The communication I had with her when our relationship first started was amazing, and the connection we had was unforgettable. Of course, the sex was excellent. She was one of the most beautiful girls I've ever met. I really fought for her to date me and then we actually started dating. She wanted to go back to California and, I guess, run again or whatever. But I think she was scared to get into a relationship, too. We did anyway and dated for about a year and a half. She stuck with me while I was going through some major shit.

I had just gotten clean and was still figuring out who I was, what I wanted, and how to act. When you get clean, your emotions don't all come back right away. Your capacity to feel love, guilt, shame, or see things from other people's points of view is damaged when you're getting high or drinking for a long time. I was still coming back to being able to feel shame and guilt. We started fighting a lot. In retrospect, I think she had some communication issues herself, and she was in a fucked-up spot, too. She had just quit drinking when we met, and she had been drinking a lot, so that was an adjustment for her. She was trying to adapt to a new area without a lot of friends or job security. Two sickies don't make a wellie.

It was hard to maintain passion when I already had issues trusting people. And we both struggled with that. It's tough rebuilding a life when you both have to do it at once. And that's really what we were trying to do. One thing I learned in that relationship with her is that I couldn't solve problems with money. When things got bad, I wanted to buy her a present, or fucking buy her dinner to make her feel better.

When I was growing up, most of my parents' problems had come down to money or finances. So, I thought I could solve the problems in our relationship with money because I was making 100 grand a year.

What I learned was from trying to buy her happiness is that people need you to relate to them, to see from their perspective, and fucking empathize. Different people like to be communicated with in different ways, and different people like to be shown love in different ways. I give love sometimes by buying things or taking my gal to go out to eat. A lot of people want a hug. That's all they really need; some emotional connection and support, and that's what Kayla craved. I couldn't give it to her at that time. I still feel bad about that. She was my first girlfriend after I got clean, so she was the first girl I could love. I still think about her.

In July of 2014, we decided to separate. We'd been living together for a little while, and she'd quit her job, and then gotten it back. It was a fucked-up scenario. So, she went back to California. We said we would spend some time apart and see what happened. In reality, it was just us ending the relationship. She fucking moved 3,000 miles away. What are we going to do? I was nuts back then. I wasn't doing any type of real personal growth work. Not doing personal growth work for me, is deadly. When I'm growing, I'm living. When I'm making progress, I'm living. Right then and there, I wasn't making any progress. I wasn't growing.

Right around the time she left, I lost my voice, and I didn't know why. I talked for a living, selling windows, so I'd have to babble on for two to four hours at a time. Not being able to speak was detrimental. I took a straight month off from work, which totally threw a wrench in my path. The year before I had been a million-dollar rep, and made the President's Club for the organization. The year I got sick, I was on track to beat my previous year by a significant margin. When I got sick, and all the relationship shit came to a head, I took it to heart, and it really fucked up my performance.

When I went to the doctor about my voice, he stated, "This is either a fluke, a weird virus, or it's the sign of serious autoimmune symptoms."

That didn't sound good, so I asked him, "How the fuck do you know whether it's an immune system issue?" He said we didn't and that we would have to wait. "If something else pops up, then we know." Eventually, my voice came back, and I returned to selling windows. But because my pay had taken such a hit from that month off, I knew I had to find some other way of generating income. I knew I had to find the next step because I needed to make more money.

A hundred grand wasn't enough anymore, and I was still digging out from missing sales. Every once in a while, I had to pay my fucking car payment late, and the rent got fucked up. I'd spent a lot of money. When I was a kid, I hadn't learned how to manage money correctly, so if I saw something I wanted, I just bought it. I knew I needed to adjust my income and lifestyle, and because I had been in sales for a few years, I also knew leveling up was possible. I could do it. If I just got into commission sales in a different industry or entrepreneurship, I would earn the type of money I dreamt about. I didn't know what kind of business I wanted to run or be a part of, but I did a lot of online research and poured through all the ads and opportunities I could find. That's when I ran into Dan, who was heavily into the real estate game, slingin' wholesale deals. Meeting Dan was the biggest professional jumping off point I had ever experienced.

Chapter 16: Getting in the Game

In October 2014, I was out to dinner with some friends when I met a guy named Dan, a person who would go on to propel me into the next phase of my life. Four mutual friends had gathered at a diner, and I asked him what he did for a living. When he said he flipped houses, he had my attention.

"Whoa, what's that? What's that mean?" He explained.

I told him my story, and about the successes I'd had selling TVs and windows and I came to learn what he really did was wholesale real estate. He said, "We put a property under contract, and then we flip the contract. So, we have to get the property between $5,000 and $20,000 below what a flipper will pay for it, which is already pretty low."

I wondered how a person could agree to such a deal and he replied, "You build a rapport. You subtly devalue the house, and then you negotiate and make them an offer." As he explained the sales process to me, I said to myself, *holy shit. That's the same thing I'm doing to sell windows, and I'm frickin' awesome at selling windows. I would be good at this.*

I was used to being the successful one in my group of friends, even though I knew there was a lot more to life than money. The next day, I hit him up and offered to buy him lunch. We went to an Italian joint called RigaTony's. They're famous for their crab cakes.

When we sat down, he explained more about the job of wholesaling real estate. I said, "I'm not really interested in doing my own marketing. What I am interested in is closing all your leads. I'll close every last one of them." He said, "All right, let's give this a shot." That's when our partnership began. He sent me the first lead that I didn't close. But you bet your ass I closed the next four. Closing four out of my first five wholesale real estate contracts, at the time, was an unheard of close rate!

Typically, a person will get one out of 10 contracts, so doing four out of five was significant, or at least it was to me. Right then and there, I set a goal that if I could make $60,000 in the next three months from those first four sales, I would quit my job and go into real estate full time. While I was getting my feet wet in real estate, I was still selling windows and running wholesale leads in my spare time. In the window business, the lead flow slows down when it gets colder outside, so the decreased demand allowed me to sell both.

I applied the same sales process to the real estate leads that I did to selling windows. First, I would warm up the buyer. A warm-up means you build rapport: "Hey, where are you from?" Conversation starters like that. Then you take a tour of the property and snap pictures. You ask how much repairs will cost and point out what needs repairing. As you're doing this, you continue to build rapport.

Ask a few closing questions like, "How soon are you looking to sell?" "What kind of price point were you thinking?" "Is anybody else looking at the property?" Then you'd make an offer, and close it. At the time, though, we weren't one-call closers. We would look at the property, get a rough construction budget, and then would check comps that night or the next day. We would make an offer within 24 hours over the phone. Once we made an offer, then we would try to solicit a counteroffer. We usually played the negotiation out until we would win the sale.

I got addicted to the hustle. I got addicted to the money. It felt like "Finally, this is what I want to do." My second or third deal was a $45,000 assignment. After we paid another wholesaler, Dan and I split 40 grand. It was one of largest assignment fees Dan had ever paid. Obviously, it was the biggest check for me, too. Immediately, as I walked out holding a check for $20,000, I thought: *Holy shit. You can get the fuck out of selling windows.*

I made $61,000 in three months and met my goal. I remember looking at that number and then at my calendar and realizing I had done it. So, I quit. In March of 2015, I stopped selling windows and went into real estate full-time. I did not know how drastically my life was about to change.

Of course, you would think from this moment on that everything would be peaches and cream and rainbows. But the reality is people always have struggles. Most people looking in from the outside don't even know what other people deal with, that they fight through every day just to make it.

Chapter 17: The Dilaudid Diaries

While I'd been balancing everything, and working my two jobs, trying to toe that stable line in life, I'd gotten sick again and again.

But life is not a situation where you just figure it all out without setbacks. I thought, *here come my struggles.*

In January, I got intensely sick and had to spend a week in the hospital once a month because I kept getting pancreatitis. I was losing weight and in pain. I couldn't eat. I was sweating. It was torture. I don't know if you've ever had pancreatitis, but it fuckin' sucks. My sickness hit when I was selling windows, and it has yet to go away. Through the telling of the rest of my story, all my wins and victories have always been accompanied by that shadow of sickness. When I was selling windows, I couldn't lift anything up for a little while because of the pain and sickness. I couldn't bring the window down for the homeowner when I went back inside the house.

In one three-month period, I juggled sickness with selling windows and closing wholesale deals with Dan. When I was in my hospital bed, I would sit there with my laptop open, and make sales calls and offers to sellers. While the nurses were drawing my blood, I was following up on sales. Just because you're sick, have an accident or go through a tragedy, it doesn't mean you have to quit. It doesn't mean you have to give up.

In fact, I took it as an opportunity to double down. I was just lying in a hospital bed, all day and instead of letting it get me down and instead of letting it hold me back, I fuckin' took it to another level. Let this fact sink in: I made more money from the hospital bed doing real estate deals than I made selling windows. I took it as a sign from the universe that it was time for me to move on (that, and that huge check I'd received). All of 2015 was rough. About once a month, I would end up in the hospital for a week with pancreatitis.

The doctors told me I had autoimmune pancreatitis, and that I was going to be in pain for the rest of my life. That my hands were going to hurt forever. Then they put me on Prednisone, and I got fat. It fucked with all my hormones, and I was miserable and depressed. But even though my body was being put through the wringer, the one thing I didn't fucking give up on was my business. The one thing I didn't quit on was fucking running the seller leads. The one thing I didn't quit on was me. I had faith in me. I had faith in the business, and I had faith that if I focused on my goals and tripled down, everything would work out for me and that's what it fuckin' did!

Enter Dilaudid, a narcotic painkiller that is more potent than heroin. It's a drug they give you in the hospital if they think you're going to die or that you have terminal cancer. The first time I got pancreatitis, I refused painkillers, and I just gritted my teeth for a week with ibuprofen and Tylenol. The second time I got pancreatitis, I did the same shit. The third time ... Motherfucker ... When I was in the hospital, you know your boy, GB took a fucking hot shot of that Dilaudid right in the middle of the night when I couldn't sleep. I don't know if you guys have ever had an IV opiate experience.

When I say "IV," I mean injected directly into your fucking vein and it is the most incredible feeling that you could ever imagine. The problem with opiates and heroin isn't that it's addictive. The problem with it is that it feels amazing. I'm talking about if God made a better feeling, then he would have kept it for himself. It's an intense, warm, rushing-over-you, cuddly feeling that infiltrates your entire body and the sensation is like you're sitting in the warmest, best bath that you could ever conjure in your mind. I hadn't had that feeling rush over me in almost three years. So, when it did, *oh, my God.* It was an absolutely-ecstatic-out-of-body abduction.

It seriously felt like my entire body was orgasming. The reason that I bring up the experience is that I'd kind of forgotten what it had been like to be high because it had been a few years. Then BOOM I could remember it. I was sick. I was making a lot of money. Making $15,000 to $30,000 a month. Reliving that feeling was not good because when I got out of the hospital boy, oh, boy, did I want to get high with a ferocious passion for a few weeks. My friend Coleen saved my ass.

She took me to a few meetings, and I cried talking about wanting to get high. I got through it. I didn't go use or buy heroin or do anything else to hurt myself. The only time I've ever been close to relapsing was after that experience. I want to talk about it because a lot of people think you just kick the habit and then it goes away forever, but it doesn't. Sometimes, that fucking monkey on your back creeps back up behind you and tries to get ahold of you. It tried to get ahold of me again.

I fought it and stayed clean, but a lot of people get caught up when they get sick and have a painkiller in the hospital. Then they're not able to control it, so they die because they relapse. Be fucking cautious.

The rest of 2015 was a transitory period. I stacked up deals, ran leads, worked with Dan and slayed. I wanted to do bigger deals and make sure our sale-getting systems were solid. I hustled seven days a week and took a step toward my goal of making more money and building a business. The first person I hired was Coleen, as a transaction coordinator.

Things didn't work out with her as an employee, which was really my fault more than anyone else's. I learned a lot of lessons through having her onboard, though. One of the takeaways I had, when she left, was: make sure you pay people on time. Make sure you take care of your employees as if they are family. Employees need to rely on you, and they need to trust you in the same way you rely on and trust them. In fact, when they feel like they can trust you as a boss—that is the most important gift you can give them. Them trusting you is even more important than whether you can trust them.

Chapter 18: Change Your State, Change Your Life

Around Christmas 2015, I bought a gift for myself: the present of coaching. Quickly, I was immersed in the world of personal improvement and growth. Calling the Tony Robbins people to set me up with a life coach, continues to be one of the best decisions I've ever made. We all have voices in the back of our head telling us that we're not good enough or deserving of being loved and we tend to see our flaws before we see our assets. We see ourselves as imperfect and therefore undesirable. Since I started working with a life coach, all that has changed for me. I see myself as worthy and take stock of the benefits I can give to others, instead of acknowledging the potential detractions and shortcomings, I perceived in myself. I cannot stress enough how truly incredible this ride has been for me. Once upon a time, I looked at my past as a problem.

I saw my past as something to be ashamed of and hidden from others, and now I know it is a badge of honor, like, "Man, I've been through some shit." If you have read this far into the fucking book, you know that, too. So, from the bottom of my heart, if you've been through some shit like I have or even just through some other kind of shit, you can get better. You can do better. You can change your life. All you have to do is change your state. Change the way you're thinking about those areas in your life that you're dissatisfied with and your entire life will change at the snap of your fingers.

In addition to the coaching, I concentrated on a few other aspects of personal growth. I attended Tony Robbins' Unleash the Power Within seminar where you walk on hot coals. Some of you guys might have heard of it already, but basically, you walk on fire. To do this, you have to get in a state. Right before you get ready to take that first step onto the coals, you slap your hands together, fucking pound your chest and go for it.

Walking across the hot coals didn't hurt at all. Tribal drums were going, and people were chanting and then all of a sudden, you fucking snap into it; you go for it and conquer your fear. You walk right across them, and it's a truly incredible feeling. Through my investment into Tony Robbins and the personal development work I did, I know I can get better. I know I can help others. I know I can be a better person each and every day. I know I can be happy. I know I deserve great things in this life and if I work for them, will get them. I know that the only difference between me and others are the actions we take and the attitude we choose to have. I don't care if you're the fucking president, a captain of industry or a homeless person. We're all just human beings, and we can have what we want if we're willing to work for it.

Chapter 19: Corporate Thuggin'

By the end of 2015, our average wholesale deal was $20,000, and it continues to hover right around that mark to this day. The reason that's important to note is the industry averages between $5,000 and $9,000. We're above average due to the sales systems we use and the way we communicate with sellers, which is a similar pattern to what we used when I was selling windows. Because of these systems, we can maintain not only a higher volume of deals, but also a higher average sales price, which translates into more revenue and more money to go around for everybody, and that's really fucking great.

In early 2016, I got a phone call from the police department in Cape May County letting me know they were charging me for the altercation in the pharmacy four and a half years ago. My response was "Motherfucker; this is like three months before the statute of limitations is up. We couldn't have handled this four years ago?!" They essentially said, "Nah, we're doing this shit now." So, I fucking had to go down, yet again, and sit in a holding cell for five hours, wearing a suit and tie, sweating without my cell phone, as they figured out whether they wanted to throw me in jail for a night for something that had happened almost five years before.

Long story short, I pleaded guilty to an attempt to obtain a controlled substance by fraud, and they gave me probation. This means I still have to make the drive and say hi to the old PO every once in a while. But fuck, I'm not in jail, and I got clean. I'm literally the poster boy for recovery at this point. Pretty fucking decent, right? Especially for me. Yeah, I was stoked about not having to go to jail. I'm not really a jail guy. Wasn't then, and I definitely am not now.

2016 was fucking boring compared to some of the other stories I've told here. I made mad loot, clocked checks. It was the same old, same old. Luckily, nothing popped up except for the ancient, ridiculous pharmacy case. All the other shit was mundane: me going out and doing the online dating thing, eating dinner at nice places and other stable shit that wasn't too bad.

In 2016, I also realized I had a business to build, and there was an opportunity for scaling something big. So, I brought on a sales guy, my boy Evan, who continues to be an absolute stallion slayer of a sales dude. He crushes deals.

He's a friend of mine from the window shop, and I had him start out making phone calls, and paying him a piece of the deal. Then, he just fucking took off and started crushing. He quit windows after working with me for a few months and. doubled his salary, which is nifty.

We brought on a transaction coordinator in January, and our deal volume doubled. Since then, we've added a couple more salespeople, Steve and Anthony. Those guys are goddamned stallions. I am so proud to go into the office every day and know that I'm working with the best in the business.

A lot of people approach real estate as a one-off business, as a one-man show. They don't have their eye on scaling. I consistently look for opportunities to scale, delegate and pull myself out of the sales process as much as I can, because the more I do that, the more we can grow, and the bigger we can get. Then the more we can help people. Those are my ultimate goals.

I take those lessons I learned selling windows, and the lessons I learned from Tony Robbins' events and watching people's videos, and I apply them to the wholesale business.

Now, we're approaching wholesale real estate as if we're a Fortune 500 Company, instead of as if we're one-off investors on the street. Every day, we get bigger. Every day, we get more efficient. Every day, we run more leads and make more money as we improve our output.

I run my business by asking myself one foundational question: "What has to get done, but doesn't have to get done.

I run my life by that question, too, and I know if I keep doing that, working from that base, that I will survive. I am going to be alright. You can borrow my question and apply it to your life to help better define your direction if you need to. (I don't mind.)

I'd love to talk to you about what I do and how it can help you find success. Head over to GeorgeBeatty.com and let's chat about wholesaling, dominating and flipping Philly.

About the Author

George Beatty is a principal with Property Pals, a multi-million-dollar real estate investor, wholesaler, property manager and sales master. A natural sales leader, since he first took his job as a telemarketer at a tender age, he now manages all aspects of real estate and has turned innovative problem-solving into consistent profitability. He and his team turn over 100 properties a year, significantly adding value to the Philadelphia market with every transaction.

A veteran of the meaner streets of Philly, George has traded fighting for his life for fighting his way up the industry ladder and has become an expert in championing for neglected properties.

In what little spare time he has, he enjoys studying jiu-jitsu and watching MMA fights. An avid cigar enthusiast, George loves reading spy thrillers as well as learning about meditation and practicing it. Every day is started with a calming moment in his mind to allow him to better seize the day and pick up where he left off...flipping Philadelphia.

George lives in Philadelphia with his tabby cat he affectionately refers to as the "Orange Prince." His trademark humor and easy-going nature are evident in all forms of his media, especially on his Facebook Live videos.

This is his first book.

Connect:

georgebeatty.com

pahouseguys.com

paoffmarket.com

diamondequityinvestments.com

facebook.com/grbeatty

paoffmarket.com

facebook.com/phillycashbuyer

Made in the USA
Middletown, DE
08 January 2018